CW01630592

My Travels in ESP – Fact, not Fiction

A Former Silva Mind Control® Instructor Shares

His Own Experience and Theories on ESP

By Richard Tamir

My Travels in ESP – Fact, not Fiction

Copyright © 2017 by Richard Tamir

Contents

PROLOGUE

We all hear about the "sixties" – really, the period from about 1965 to 1975. Everything was wild and crazy. Hippies, demonstrations, social unrest.

There was something else about the sixties that went mostly unnoticed. In 1966, the first ever course that trained ESP – Extra Sensory Perception, or parapsychology, and including telepathy and clairvoyance – was developed. And it worked: at the end of the course, every student tried a double-blind experiment to "see" information they had never experienced before. And to verify that information at the source, later on. This was the Silva Mind Control® course, later renamed to The Silva Process® and other tradenames, invented by Jose Silva.

The Silva Course combined many past self-development courses – plus a bit more in the area of psychic functioning – into a single, straight-through training that took 4 evenings or a full weekend. It took all applicants, and every one of them had a high probability of proving that their skills worked. I was a student of that course, in its original form, in 1969. It was what we called then "mind-blowing" – not in the course content, but what it revealed about our capabilities as human beings. This was stuff that was natural – we only needed to learn how to make it work.

I was so enthralled with the results that I eventually became an instructor, teaching in Northern Florida. My journey to becoming an instructor was a bit "out of the box", as you will read, and many, many of my experiences were also unusual.

Since my background was scientific, I applied my own quasi-scientific rules to these experiences. For those of you who think this is all voodoo, it isn't: there are rules that apply, and there is even an underlying theory or model (or perhaps many of them beyond my own) that can help gain understanding. My goals were simple:

1. Explore this new world of ESP, and
2. Try to find some logical way to understand it.

I believe I succeeded at both. The ideas I developed were different from most theories of the day, but identical to a few philosophers' ideas, so I knew that I was on the right track. I also found that most folks really were nervous or afraid around this subject, at least until they took the Silva course. So I developed a third goal, which I also achieved:

3. Find a way to understand ESP that takes away the fear. Since this fear itself can prevent people from doing the right steps to succeed in ESP functioning, just this alone will increase the number of people who are successful in this area.

This book goes as far back as the beginning in 1966, and as far forward as today. It presents what I experienced, many of which were extraordinary events, and my thinking on how they fit together with our current ideas of the universe and its principles. And, on my oath, they are all true and personally experienced.

I hope you enjoy reading this. Definitely try out the instructions. They are all simple, they all work, and the experiences you will have are your own and will be real.

1968 – STUMBLING ONTO THE SILVA COURSE

At this time, I was a computer programmer living in Berkeley, California. I rented a house with two other guys, and once in a while we found something we were all interested in. One of the roommates, a math professor, came home one day and said he had found an interesting advertisement for a course that taught ESP. Since I was an avid science fiction fan from the age of 10, I was definitely interested. The other roommate, an Emergency Room physician, was also interested. So we went to the public seminar where the course was being promoted, to see what it was.

We walked in interested, and walked out laughing. The claims they made!!! Better memory, better health, higher chances of winning games of chance, better religious experiences – and it went on and on. Too much! So we forgot about ESP.

A year later, I moved back to my native home in Boston, Massachusetts. I was now a science teacher at a military-base middle school. I had forgotten about the Silva Course, but it came up in discussion during a visit to some old family friends. Sally Mlavsky, a woman more than ten years my senior, was interested in our visit to the Silva seminar, and at the end of the story said simply, "You might try it out. It works." I was a bit stunned by that, but trusted Sally's judgment implicitly. So I found the local Silva course through its newspaper ad, and went to their seminar. And then I took the course.

What was this course? It was an unusual combination of what seemed to be different things, but which (as I later saw) were all necessary to achieve psychic functioning. Please note that this book will not be about Silva Mind Control, except as a stepping stone to the psychic experiences that happened, then and later. Those experiences, and my ideas and thoughts about them, are the core of this book.

TAKING THE COURSE

Having attended the nearly-identical seminar to the one in San Francisco, I simply paid my money to take the course. I applied no judgment, since I had the recommendation of a trusted friend. (A detailed description of the course (Silva Life Systems Curriculum) appears as Appendix A.)

The following description is intentionally informal, leaving out much of the detail shown in the appendix.

The course had four half-day sessions. The content included the following information, which is slightly out of order for easier explanation. The correct order is shown in the Appendix.

Silva course, session one:

- First, we learned how to physically relax. This involved deep breathing, and later learning to tense and relax muscles "from the top to the bottom" of our bodies. Many of us fell asleep, but the instructor said that was fine – our minds were taking in all the instructions we were given.
- Then we learned a bit of imagination: seeing our relaxation stages as going down a stairway, with various landings along the way. Each landing downward was a deeper stage of relaxation that the one before. (Yes, this is also used in hypnosis.)
- Once at our "final stage of relaxation", we were given instructions on how to get back to that level easily any time that we wanted.
- Note that I've left out a few exercises, such as memory training using the "memory pegs" system. This had no lasting importance for the ESP aspects of the course, but was helpful in getting people to form images in their minds.
- This was the end of the first phase of our ESP education.

Silva course, session two:

- The second stage became much more "woo-woo" or borderline strange. We went to the final stage of relaxation, and then – in our minds – imagined various things. First it was just a piece of fruit, which we examined with our (inner) vision, taste, smell and (for some things) hearing.
- We "built" a laboratory in our mind. This lab had all sorts of imaginary tools in it, from things that were medically standard up to anything we could imagine might be useful.

- In one of the stranger training sessions, we met our "Counselors" in the laboratory. A panel came down in a wall, revealing an imaginary person who would help us when we needed help. We did this twice, and at the end of the session we all had a male Counselor and a female Counselor.
    - For a brief discussion of the laboratory and counselors, see http://mylifepuzzle.com/2012/03/07/mind-laboratory-and-counselors-silva-life-system/
- This was the end of the second phase of the course.

Silva course, session three:

- In day three, we "learned" about anatomy of the human body. No medical student would ever have an easier course – it was at a top-level of detail only, used many simple pictures and cartoons during the lecture phase, then all of these were reemphasized during our training sessions when we were all "at our level". (Basically, we were all lying down with our eyes closed, listening to the instructor's words.)
- We not only saw the normal, healthy human body, but certain signs of ill health were described during the training session. For example, ill health could be seen as black spots on a certain organ. (Sounds pretty basic, huh?)
- By the end of the third day, we were all ready for Day Four – *Doing It!*

Silva course, session four:

- Day Four was different from the other days. After teaching the final and necessary skills for doing Health Cases (see below), most of the time was spent testing out our newly found powers – which none of us believed we had!
- The way this was conducted was fully "double-blind": in each psychic reading, neither the person asking questions nor the person "at their level" and psychically answering them, knew

anything about the subject of the experiment. So, properly done, there was no way to cheat on this stuff. Here's the way it happened:

- First, everyone was asked to get some 3" X 5" cards (supplied) and write a "health case" on anyone they know or are related to. Health was the focus and therefore people with illness were chosen to focus on, and perhaps try to help.
- On the front of the card we'd put the name / age / sex / city of the person in question. On the back, we'd write a short description of the health problems they were facing at that time. Any detail was welcome – source of problem (e.g., auto accident), prognosis if known, etc. these were all on the back of the card. Then all of the cards, typically 3-4 times the number of people in the room, were put on a table with the card's identity side facing up and visible.
- Then all students formed into pairs. Each pair would have two roles to play: the questioner and the answerer. The questioner held the card in their hands, the answerer was at their level with eyes closed. The role of the questioner was to ask questions that would keep the psychic or answerer involved in the conversation, and especially not falling asleep. (Easy to do when you are "at your level".) One important point: the questions were not supposed to lead the subject to known health problems; the most directive they should be would be to suggest "probing deeper" or using tools in their laboratory or asking their Guides questions as to the meaning of what they saw in their minds.
- The questioner would take notes on the comments made, and after the "health case" was finished, both would compare the results with the data on the back of the cards. Further information could also be obtained by asking the author of the card, whose name was included.

- Although some questioners suggested answers, most were skillful in asking only neutral, non-leading questions. This was critical in establishing the success of the health case reading, assuming that there were accurate facts discovered. And there were, frequently.
- Once a health case was finished, the cards went back to the main table, the questioner and answerer changed roles, and the next case was done. During the course of the last day's session, each student performed as many as six cases in each role.

DOING MY FIRST CASE

Here's what happened: I was given the case of an elderly lady currently under medical care. Going "to my level", I could see within five minutes that she had "triglyceride problems", even though I had no idea what that meant. (And this was correct.) I found other issues, identified them and moved on. Then, as I got deeper into the case, I had the impression that I could "see" where she lived. It was very clear: a typical boarding-house room with a bed, night table, sink, mirror, calendar, window, etc. We ended the case with my "sending energy" for her to get better, as we did with all cases, and then I came up through my levels, opened my eyes and started speaking with my questioner. Thankfully, she had not led me with any of her questions, so I felt that my observations were fairly obtained.

We went through the results, comparing what I said with what the card said. Nothing was in conflict, and I had seen most of the major issues on the (originally hidden) back of the card. The questioner could have looked at that information and probably did, but her questions gave no suggestions for me to follow.

Then we discussed the room I had seen the subject living in. The questioner had no way of knowing whether the image in my mind was accurate, since this was not her card or her family member. I was curious to verify what I saw, and we sought out the card's author. When I described the room to her, she said, "No, she didn't live alone. She had a husband and they lived in a single-family house." This was a disappointment for me, since I had clearly seen this boarding-house room. Then the author asked me a question: "When was it that she was living there?" I said I had no idea. She thought a moment, then asked if I would be willing to go "back to my level", re-image that room and look closely at the calendar on the wall; she wanted to see the date. So that's what I did, and the calendar showed September 1969; our course was happening two months later. When I said September, the relative of the subject exclaimed, "Oh my God! Her husband had a heart attack and went into the hospital for a one-month period. She couldn't take care of the house by herself, so she lived briefly in a boarding house – and it was this past September." I looked at her directly, she looked at me, and we both nearly fainted. In my first case, I had seen accurate information beyond the knowledge of the questioner, and also beyond the written data *and immediate knowledge* of the card's author. And the data I saw was accurate.

I was dumbfounded: not only was my first case accurate, it was "beyond accurate". I had to leave the room. My mind felt it would split out of my head. I was amazed, I was stupefied – but I had definitely succeeded in achieving something extraordinary. ***Seeing something that I had no possible way of knowing beforehand – the definition of clairvoyance!***

WHAT WAS THE MEANING OF THIS EXPERIENCE?

One of the most basic principles of an ESP experience is that it is *an inner experience*. No one in the room around you had that experience, only you did. No one in the room, or listeners / readers of this story later on, can be assured that I was not lying. With Aristotelian standards of experimentation – that is, the true "scientific method" – all experimentation must be observable by independent third parties, to eliminate the possibility of charlatans making wild and unscientific claims.

With ESP experiments, however, there is a universal characteristic: they are "inner experiences", ones that you know you had and others have no way of confirming. This is against principles of scientific method, and is the key reason that ESP is considered non-scientific.

But I knew what I experienced. I wasn't lying to myself. And thankfully, based on the experimental design built into the Silva "health case" test at the end of the course, others had observed how I obtained the information. (Of course, this does not protect against the entire health case being a stage act – only I could know that it wasn't, with full certainty.)

What had this experience proven?

1. ESP exists: I could see information I had no experience with. Clairvoyance.
2. Other skills now could also exist: telepathy, precognition, even telekinesis.
3. The world I was taught to accept is not the complete truth – there is more.
4. This is teachable to others, since a few moments ago I was an "other".
5. Finally, I didn't have to give up the science fiction dreams of my childhood – here they were, right in front of me.

Accepting all of this, of course, was another story. My mind swirled with the changes and their implications. Now, to be responsible to myself, I had to learn more – what was easily available, going beyond the structured health cases, finding others to work with, etc., etc.

As you might expect, I was excited by all this. I wanted to experience it again, and get to know others who were going through the same transition. The Silva Course offered nothing except an "advanced course" that would travel through Boston a few months later. So a few of us decided to get together informally, practice some health cases and perhaps do experiments beyond those.

The name we gave these practice sessions was "cottage groups", and they travelled from home to home every two weeks. A lot of new experiences happened there.

COTTAGE GROUPS

Since the cottage groups were not under Silva Mind Control auspices, we were completely free to conduct the groups as we wished. This was the structure that developed over time:

1. We would all sit down, join hands, and participate in an "energy circle". This required all of us to go to our level (meditate briefly to relax our minds and bodies). Once we joined hands, we would imagine a ball of energy in the middle of the circle; we would pass it along the circle in one direction, then the other, always making the size and brightness of the circle grow. (Remember, this was the sixties.) At the end, when the circle was very large and bright, we would each imagine people who needed help from this energy – the subjects of health cases we had done in the past, our families and friends, and people in need of improved health that we knew about. Then we ended the energy circle and started working health cases.
2. The health cases were now gathered from our personal acquaintances. They were family and friends of ours, or of our own family and friends. We actively requested these cases for practice and people were generous in supporting us with new health cases.
3. At the end of each cottage group meeting, we held a second energy circle, again sending healing energy to those we knew or had treated.
4. We kept the old health cases from meeting to meeting, to have a backlog for future meetings to work with and to find out if any

improvement had happened. Unfortunately, this sometimes meant that an earlier health case had passed, or died, in the meantime. Typically, death was seen as a grey color on the imagined body. We found this to be an accurate signal for a person no longer living.

With practice, our skills became stronger. Some of us, we found, were more visual in seeing data, some of us "felt it" by using our hands in the air in front of our faces – as if we were conducting a medical examination. Some actually heard different sounds that became their signals for various health conditions. The accuracy was high, and getting better with each meeting.

DOING A PUBLIC DEMO

One day I received a call from Chris Jensen, the New England Regional Director for Silva. He was giving a sales seminar for the course the next week, and wondered if I could come and help him with a "demo case". I hadn't seen a demo case before, but didn't see why it should not work, so I said yes.

At the sales seminar, there were perhaps 100 attendees with the same questions I had had before taking the course. Chris asked them if they would like to see a case done in front of them, and they were quite excited about that.

Chris acted as my questioner in this health case. After the initial deepening exercises bringing me to my level, he identified a specific person to look at. So I did what we had been taught: I put him "on the screen" in my laboratory, did various examinations, found various items of ill health and reported them to Chris. And Chris, by the way, was scrupulous in not leading me with his questions: what I saw came from my own initiative.

The major points of this health case were concerned with this man's throat; apparently he was a heavy smoker and was now paying the health price. After I had given Chris all the information I could determine, he asked me if I would like to "put on his head". This is a technique where the psychic reaches out with his / her hands to the sides of the imagined head on their laboratory screen, picks it up and fits it over their own head. It can be very effective in feeling symptoms from a distance, but not being affected by them painfully or dangerously.

When I put on the head, I settled in my seat and let the feelings permeate me. I felt certain neck and throat muscles shift and change their characteristic pattern. I told this to Chris, who suggested I let it proceed a moment more and then speak to him in the voice of the health case subject.

The rest of the health case, perhaps 5-10 minutes, was spent with me answering questions in my imagined voice of the subject, based on the muscles in my throat that had tensed up. Then Chris ended the session, we sent energy to this man, and I brought myself back to the surface – i.e., out of my level. Then I opened my eyes and looked at the audience in front of me.

Unbelievable: I saw a wall of faces showing utter astonishment, even a few in shock. The ones in shock were the relatives and friends of the subject case. Why? Because when I started speaking in his voice as I imagined it, which was quite different from my own voice, they heard his actual voice come out. It had all the roughness, timbre, tone and other characteristics of this gentleman's voice, as affected by his health condition. To them this was amazing, even a bit frightening – but they had witnessed it and it was real. I told them I had never done such an exercise before and appreciated their letting me know the accuracy of the technique. Then I went to another room, sat down and thought a lot about what had happened.

I had not "become" this other man; I had simply allowed his imagined body to work as part of mine. And yet, it created an accurate sound picture of the man we were studying. This was another form of clairvoyance, except it went beyond seeing. And I had less and less doubt that the energy we sent might be able to have an effect on our case subjects. After all, if I can be affected by him (the new voice), then perhaps he can be affected by me (an improved health situation). Evidence was building that we were onto something really important.

HAVING AN EFFECT ON OUR HEALTH CASE SUBJECTS

As our cottage groups continued and advanced, we found that we had no feedback on the work we were doing. Yes, we sent "healing energy" to others at the beginning and end of our sessions – but what good did they do? We had no way of knowing – at least, until the following situation happened:

Our group was composed of very respectable people. It was a mix of society, all intensely interested in exploring the world of ESP. There were rich and middle-class, even one or two poor who could find transportation; we were Christian and Jewish; we were old and young.

One of the most established and respected members of the group was Henry Hosmer and his wife. They were pure Yankee stock, he worked in one of the top Boston law firms, and had the "crusty" personality that many old-line attorneys seemed to take. Yet Henry was very approachable and warm once initial barriers were surmounted.

Henry and his wife participated in nearly all our cottage groups. They, like me, had come to the Silva course as skeptics and had been bowled over by the results of the course. They were curious to learn more, and the cottage group was the best available tool. No books could impart the personal experiences we sought.

After many meetings, Henry came to us with a request at the energy circle one night. He had a sister named Daisy who had suffered for years from very painful and debilitating arthritis; it severely affected her life. Daisy had seen many doctors and had been prescribed many drugs. Nevertheless, her pain continued to increase. Earlier that day, her doctor had informed her that he could not increase her prescription strength for her increasing pain, since she was already at the maximum dose. Daisy was extremely disheartened, and suffering a lot.

Naturally, all the members of the cottage group sent Daisy healing energy in our usual way, although perhaps the ball of energy was larger and brighter than usual given the very personal relationship we had with Henry. Daisy, by the way, knew nothing of Henry's Silva training, his interest in ESP, or our meetings as a cottage group.

At the next meeting, two weeks later, Henry reported the following:

- Daisy called him a week later. She related that her pain started to decrease without any explanation, starting the morning after our cottage group – which she knew nothing about.
- Day by day, her pain decreased. As a result, she started decreasing her medication dosage.
- A week after the cottage group, Daisy stopped all medications and had no pain from her arthritis.
- Daisy was baffled by this turn of events, but absolutely thrilled to have escaped the pain she had been suffering.

Henry then told Daisy about the Silva course, the cottage group meetings, and our last meeting's sending of energy to her personally. She was surprised, since this was not the Henry she knew and had grown up with. But she couldn't argue with the success she experienced in loss of pain.

Daisy Hosmer enrolled as a student at the next Silva course. As far as I know, her pain never returned.

LIFE REGRESSIONS – EXPLORING OTHER LIVES

The cottage group format was simple, repetitive and sometimes boring. We looked for other work we could do during the meetings, and one of us suggested "life regressions". I had no familiarity with these, and learned that they were psychic (maybe) explorations of other lives. They could have simply been imagination, since it was very hard to confirm information received in these sessions.

Here's how a life regression was done:

1. The subject (here, the person doing the regression) would lie down on a couch and go to their level, as described above. There would also be a guide, performing the same role as the questioner in the health cases. Neither of them had any idea or knowledge of the persons whose lives would be viewed during the regression. (In fact, those persons were entirely unknown – they just happened to us.)
2. Once the subject was relaxed and at their level, the guide would suggest that they envision themselves in their home – perhaps a bedroom, living room, wherever. Typically, or by suggestion if necessary, the subject would imagine themselves floating above the room level, looking down.
3. Then the suggestion was made that the subject make their "spirit body" lighter, and to float up through the house/apartment and up to the roof. Then look around and describe their surroundings. These descriptions were usually quite detailed and accurate.
4. Then the suggestion was made to get "even lighter" and float upwards to, say, 500 feet. Then to look around and describe the surroundings again. Typically, there was less detail and a broader perspective on the area around them.
5. The same procedure took the subject to 1,000 feet, 10,000 feet, 50,000 feet – and then into space above the earth. Each time

they were asked to described their surroundings, in particular looking down at the earth.

6. Once in space, the suggestion was made to slowly make themselves heavier and go back down to earth at a reasonable rate, feet first, and "into another life". When they reached the earth and touched ground, they would be in another life and should let the guide know.
7. Once that happened, the guide suggested, "Look at your feet." This may seem unusual but was actually very effective, since the feet being viewed were invariably different from the subject's own feet. They might be feet of the opposite sex, might have old-style shoes, etc.
8. Then the guide suggested that the subject look around them and describe what they saw in their mind. With this approach, details were generally clearly seen and the vista was generally different from the subject's own life.
9. Then the life regression began in earnest. More and more detailed questions were asked; the subject was asked to move backward in time to the childhood period, forward in time to adulthood or old age, etc. At every step, questions were asked for details on what was being seen. The life was fully viewed, or as much as was possible within a brief time span (30-45 minutes).
10. For many life regressions (in my case as a guide, for all of them), the subject was directed forward in the viewed life up to the last moments of life. Many death scenes were similar when relatives were involved; sometimes, accidents were involved and were highly individual. Again, more questions on the details were asked.
11. Finally, and most important for reasons discussed later, the subject was asked to report on the scene both during and after the death of that person. Frequently, when the life regression continued after death, an astonishing thing happened: nearly

all the descriptions were the same. And none of the subjects had been given any details about this procedure in advance.

12. What did the subjects see? They saw the same information that had been reported in serious medical research on patients who died on the operating table, yet survived and came back to life. These reports have been thoroughly researched, and are described in the next paragraph.

What did I see? And what was reported to me by participants whom I guided? My own observations were uniform across all life regressions I did, at least those where a death was involved and we could observe the subject during that death:

- Our viewpoint was from a diagonal position upward. We looked down upon the scene, typically a deathbed scene with relatives around the bed. There were other types of scenes, but not as frequently.
- We could see the subject on the bed below us. We could observe the conversations going on, and then we saw the subject pass over into death. We saw the reactions of the relatives and friends, then they passed out of the room.
- The subject himself/herself had died, but his/her essence was still in the room. My perspective changed from that of an external observer looking at the subject, to being the subject looking down at himself. Quite possibly, my perspective had always been as the subject, even before the death – then I (my real self) was simply observing the subject observing himself. (This makes more sense to me.)
- The subject would remain in the room or the house, or the immediate area of the death, for a time after the death had completed and the friends and relatives had paid their respects. Then, alone, the subject would contemplate the scene for a while (anywhere from a few minutes to days).

- Then the subject "detached mentally" from the scene, from the relatives and friends, and from his or her own physical body. They would rise away from the scene, often seeing a tunnel around them; but always, they were moving toward a light they could see in the distance.
- This light was yellowish-white and very strong and clear. The closer the subject came, the brighter it became, although there was no source visible.
- At a certain point, the subject simply merged into this light and became part of it. All imagery for the subject disappeared – he or she had maintained the image of their human form up until then. Now they merged into the infinity of that light and, having done so, lost all physical connections. They were "part of the light", and that was the end of their life regression as far as we could see.
- Please note that similar-to-identical experiences were reported in life regressions I led, and which others led. No one was pre-advised as to what they` might see. All experiences were original and unbiased. I include here experiences that did not involve me at all, to ensure there is no impression that I influenced the outcomes, consciously or not.

In the very first book about "near death experiences" in 1975, Dr. Raymond Moody documented the experiences of 150 patients. His webpage is at http://www.near-death.com/science/experts/raymond-moody.html. Dr. Moody's book started an entirely new area of medical research, which can be seen by Googling "near death experiences" or going to Amazon.com with the same inquiry. Below is content from Dr. Moody, dating from his first research in 1975:

Dr. Moody recorded and compared the experiences of 150 persons who died, or almost died, and then recovered. His research describes the results of decades of inquiry into the NDE phenomenon. He outlines nine elements that generally occur during NDEs.

Dr. Raymond Moody's Nine Elements of the Near-Death Experiences:

1. **A Strange Sound:** A buzzing, or ringing noise, while having a sense of being dead.
2. **Peace and Painlessness:** While people are dying, they may be in intense pain, but as soon as they leave the body the pain vanishes and they experience peace.
3. **Out-of-Body Experience:** The dying often have the sensation of rising up and floating above their own body while it is surrounded by a medical team, and watching it down below, while feeling comfortable. They experience the feeling of being in a spiritual body that appears to be a sort of living energy field.
4. **The Tunnel Experience:** The next experience is that of being drawn into darkness through a tunnel, at an extremely high speed, until reaching a realm of radiant golden-white light. Also, although they sometimes report feeling scared, they do not sense that they were on the way to hell or that they fell into it.
5. **Rising Rapidly into the Heavens:** Instead of a tunnel, some people report rising suddenly into the heavens and seeing the Earth and the celestial sphere as they would be seen by astronauts in space.
6. **People of Light:** Once on the other side of the tunnel, or after they have risen into the heavens, the dying meet people who glow with an inner light. Often they find that friends and relatives who have already died are there to greet them.
7. **The Being of Light:** After meeting the people of light, the dying often meet a powerful spiritual being whom some have identified as God, Jesus, or some religious figure.

8. **The Life Review:** The Being of Light presents the dying with a panoramic review of everything they have ever done. That is, they relive every act they have ever done to other people and come away feeling that love is the most important thing in life.
9. **Reluctance to Return:** The Being of Light sometimes tells the dying that they must return to life. Other times, they are given a choice of staying or returning. In either case, they are reluctant to return. The people who choose to return do so only because of loved ones they do not wish to leave behind.

Source: http://www.near-death.com/science/experts/raymond-moody.html

Dr. Moody's experience is shown above. My personal observations are shown below, following his numbering and descriptions:

2. **Peace and Painlessness:** While people are dying, they may be in intense pain, but as soon as they leave the body the pain vanishes and they experience peace.
3. **Out-of-Body Experience:** The dying often have the sensation of rising up and floating above their own body while it is surrounded by a medical team, and watching it down below, while feeling comfortable. They experience the feeling of being in a spiritual body that appears to be a sort of living energy field.
4. **The Tunnel Experience:** The next experience is that of being drawn into darkness through a tunnel, at an extremely high speed, until reaching a realm of radiant golden-white light. Also, although they sometimes report feeling scared, they do not sense that they were on the way to hell or that they fell into it.
5. **Rising Rapidly into the Heavens:** Instead of a tunnel, some people report rising suddenly into the heavens and seeing the Earth and the celestial sphere as they would be seen by astronauts in space.
9. **Reluctance to Return:** The Being of Light sometimes tells the dying that they must return to life. Other times, they are given a

choice of staying or returning. In either case, **they are reluctant to return. The people who choose to return do so only because of loved ones they do not wish to leave behind.**

In my own experience, items 1, 6, 7 and 8 were rarely seen. However, the circumstances were different: Dr. Moody's patients actually went through real death. Therefore, I find these differences understandable. **But most importantly, it is the similarities that are most remarkable to me.**

COMMENTARY: Seeing essentially identical results in life regression subjects, when viewing the death experience, was more than remarkable. It apparently revealed a truth that we were never taught. And, to be sure, I checked with others in my region regarding their own experiences as guides and subjects, and these were the same. (I estimate the number of life regressions I conducted as over 50; and I experienced over 5as a subject.}

Going through a life regression as a subject is almost surreal, almost more real than real. The life you are viewing unrolls like a movie, and you can wind it backward and forward. You don't control the content, you view it. As the life gets older, you see changes due to aging – health, relationships, personal concerns (you can feel the person's own feelings). It is a super-movie, and very clear in your mind once you start the viewing process.

Again, life regressions were not part of the Silva course. The Silva course gave me a "ticket to ride", and then I chose which rides I wanted. Of all of them, I found life regressions the most valuable. They introduced new experiences to my own world view and explained many supernatural views held worldwide: life after death, ideas about reincarnation, the transmigration of souls, and more. All Eastern religions believe in this except Islam, and most Western religions have a significant number of sects that adhere to this belief. My question until doing the life regressions was ***Why?*** Where was the evidence? And here I saw it for my own eyes (as subject), and through others' eyes (as guide, and indirectly through the testimony of other guides and subjects). This was more than "significant" – it was massively important.

There was one area, however, where my observations and resulting belief differed from most others. That was the question of Identity. Did Person A become Person B? Or did Person A's "life force" simply move on, commingle with the life forces of other living beings, and then a new soul would be created? My observations favored the second interpretation, and this meant that Person A had no link with the identity of Person B. To me and many others, this is an important point since it affects questions of personal responsibility for past and future lives; other issues are also affected.

Further discussion on reincarnation will appear in this book. The reader is also recommended to review the Wikipedia article on Reincarnation (https://en.wikipedia.org/wiki/Reincarnation), showing the broad belief in this concept among many religions and the differences between them. If interested in further reading, there are hundreds of serious books – both secular and religious – on the subject.

In summary, I had found an area of study with significant importance. The Silva course was not an end in itself, but it did give the tools to pursue other areas of interest in the "non-Aristotelian" universe. I decided to become an instructor.

BECOMING AN INSTRUCTOR

This became a sequence of attending many Silva courses, helping the instructor as needed, and sometimes conducting training sessions when the instructor felt confident in me. The training sessions involved reading from the Silva instructor's book, which had every training session printed in full length. The sessions each included a review of past training, further deepening instructions to ensure good meditative levels, and then guided learning on new content to be taught in that session.

Jose Rodriguez was my mentor during this time, and he and I conducted many courses jointly. He was a delightful teacher and helped me understand better the structure of the Silva course. These sessions also gave me a strong class presence, which is helpful when dealing with students with questions, sometimes even problems, with what we were teaching them.

The expected result of training under a licensed instructor was a recommendation to Chris Jensen, the New England Regional Director, to be sent to Laredo, Texas for full instructor training.

Alas, that was not the path chosen for me.

THE SILVA INSTRUCTORS' COURSE

As it turned out, Chris Jensen was anti-Semitic and I am Jewish. Bad combination, and one that led to my application to become a Silva instructor being rejected. There were now many Silva-imitative courses available (Mind Dynamics®, for one), but I wanted the original Silva Course taught by Jose Silva himself. Accept no substitutions, as they say.

So, when the time came for the official training course, I simply purchased an airplane ticket and few to Laredo. No telling what might happen, but not trying was not an option.

As it turned out, Chris' rejection of my application meant little. Harry McKnight, Jose's operational control guy, simply suggested that I find a sponsor – and quickly. Class was about to start.

I found a sponsor within a half hour: Shelley Silverman was Regional Director for Florida, and he sponsored my training. Shelley also was Jewish and understood both my New England situation and my intense drive to instruct the course.

Our agreement was that, after training, I would move to Gainesville, Florida (Home of the Gators!!) and instruct in the following locations:

1. Gainesville, Florida
2. Ocala, Florida
3. Palatka, Florida
4. St. Augustine, Florida
5. Valdosta, Georgia

And thus started my career as a certified Silva Mind Control Instructor®.

STORY: THE MASSACHUSETTS LOTTERY

While I was studying to be an instructor, there was a big event happening in Massachusetts. After years of Blue Laws dating back to the 1600s and a Puritan influence, Massachusetts was finally going to have its own lottery. And it was quite late, compared to other states.

The lottery was being discussed everywhere, so I guess it was on my mind also. The night before the lottery began, I even had a dream about it – and I'm a person who never dreams, or never remembers his dreams. Surprisingly, my dream showed me some numbers! So, always attentive to the possibilities of the mind, I woke up and wrote those numbers down.

In the morning, I called the lottery and asked how I could buy a particular number. The answer was that I couldn't – at that time, the lottery numbers were printed on tickets and purchased only with numbers pre-printed. Today you can choose a number, but then you could not.

Even without the possibility of buying a number, I wanted to see whether "my numbers" were winners. What was the result? You judge for yourself:

- The lottery numbers at that time were between 0 and 99.
- Six numbers were drawn.
- Anyone who was correct in both the numbers and in the order of their drawing would win $1,000,000.

For simplicity, I'll call each number by A, B, C, etc. Each letter stands for a number between 0 and 99.

Here were the numbers I wrote down from my dream:

A B C D E F

Here are the numbers that were drawn in the order they were drawn:

A B C D F E

Nobody got the prize that first drawing. But the numbers I saw were 100% correct! The order in which I remembered them was not – I got the last two numbers reversed. So, under the rules of the day, I would not have won the $1 million prize. But what if I had remembered better, what if the lottery number could then be chosen by the ticket holder, what if…., what if….

More significantly perhaps, the accuracy of seeing the correct six numbers out of 6 is so far the only precognitive experience I have had. Precognition is knowing something before it has happened, and to my mind it is the rarest of psychic skills; only telekinesis ranks beyond it.

Precognition requires that we see time differently, negate the three-dimensional world all around us, and accept that we can cross the "timeline" of past / present / future events as if we were floating above the plane.

I welcome the opportunity for more precognitive successes, but haven't seen it since 1971.

And yes, all the experiences I relate in this book are true.

TEACHING SILVA CLASSES IN FLORIDA

To begin with, I should reveal my end results for your information. I taught 188 students during these classes – not a lot by Silva standards, since most instructors came from a high-pressure sales background and a few earned millions. But I built my territory and instructed these students, and was happy to do so.

The Silva course included a student satisfaction, money-back guarantee. This enabled those who did not succeed with their cases to leave without any hard feelings, if they so desired. (Most did not leave, but stayed and tried again in the next course.) Of the 188 students, the money-back guarantee was claimed once, by 2 people training together: a mother and daughter pair, where the daughter was in a terminal illness situation. Given her health problems, I personally worked with the daughter in her final session to ensure that it was correctly done, and that she hopefully succeeded with her cases. Based on what she reported during the session, she did succeed – but her health situation and depression kept her from believing it. Her money was fully refunded without question.

So, looking at this 98.94% success rate, what did the students learn? And what did I learn?

WHAT DID THE STUDENTS LEARN?

For this question, I won't repeat everything I've described already. Instead, I will quote from a psychiatric study of the Silva Course entitled, "Silva Mind Control and the Psychiatric Patient"; authors CLANCY D. MCKENZIE, M.D., and LANCE s. WRIGHT, MJ. This paper is reprinted in full in the book, "The Silva Mind Control Method" co-authored by Jose Silva and Philip Miele. (Currently available online, including the study, at https://spidercatweb.files.wordpress.com/2017/02/jose-silva-the-silva-mind-control-method.pdf)

The paper was originally intended as a formal study of how much harm the Silva Course caused to psychotic patients. Soon into the program, the experimenters saw little harm, but much good; therefore, some of the protocols were changed accordingly. You can read the full paper online at the URL quoted above, as Appendix II at page 182.

In their paper, the authors wrote the following description of the Silva Course:

> **What is Silva Mind Control?**
>
> Silva Mind Control is a forty-hour course consisting of
>
> thirty hours of lecture and ten hours of mental exercises.
>
> The mental exercises not only teach persons how to relax
>
> the mind and body, as do other approaches such as biofeedback
>
> and Transcendental Meditation, but they go one
>
> step beyond. They teach persons how to function mentally

when they are at the relaxed level.

The entire course consists of techniques for using the mind in beneficial ways. After experiencing this ourselves and witnessing many others using it, we have no doubt about the superior ability of the mind to function when the person is using specific techniques in an alert relaxed state.

It is similar to the state Sigmund Freud described in his paper on listening; like the state Brahms went into for creating his compositions, or the state Thomas Edison described for arriving at new ideas.

The course teaches a quick, easy method for going to this level of relaxation at any time. Trainees practice visualizing, imagining, and thinking at this level of consciousness, until they learn to function there mentally. They capture a

wider range of brain activity for conscious use. They have

an expanded range of consciousness. Instead of just daydreaming

when they are relaxed, they can use their minds

effectively at that level. Instead of being in a light slumber,

they can have awareness and use of the mind at that level

too. Instead of just dreaming at night, they can use the

dream state to solve problems and arrive at answers the

mind is not capable of at any other time.

When persons learn to function mentally at the deeper

levels of relaxation of mind and body, creativity is enhanced.

Memory is improved, and persons are better able

to solve problems. From the altered state, they are able to

direct the mind to do what they desire, and thus control of

such habits as smoking is made easier.

All students took the same course. For many, doors were opened to further practice or study, as happened in my own case. In Gainesville, we formed a cottage group similar to the one I joined in New England, and we did similar exercises. Although not every graduate was enthused enough to do follow-on activities, all the graduated students were positive about their experience.

WHAT DID I LEARN?

As instructor, I believe that I learned far more than I taught to others. Remember that I wanted to expand my understanding of these phenomena through extensive experience, which instructing gave me.

All my skills improved. They improved to the point that they became subconscious and in constant operation – that is, I did not have to initiate each and every use of a technique. They simply became part of my observation of the world around me. Some were basic interpersonal skills, such as understanding questions and needs in class. Some, however, went beyond this:

STORY: WHERE'S RUTH?

Just as I had become a student-in-training with Jose Rodriquez in Boston, Ruth Fort became a student-in-training with me. She was intensely interested in the course and techniques, and wanted to learn as much as possible. She became the informal leader of the cottage group, and was active at all our events.

Then she suddenly was gone. No one knew where, and our efforts to find her failed. I was disappointed, but knew that Ruth was a private person with her own life issues, and possibly would be back.

In addition to the Gainesville course, I also taught elsewhere. About 3 months later, I taught a course in Ocala Florida four evenings during a week. Each night at the end of class, I had a 45-minute drive back to my apartment in Gainesville, going north on interstate 75 and then east on Florida 24. The state route was then mainly undeveloped, passing only a small strip mall before reaching my new apartment complex. This featured a restaurant, liquor store and Big Daddy's Bar (famous to all Floridians at the time). The design was ingenious – the bar was attached to the back side of the liquor store.

Monday night I drove north on 75, then east on 24. As I was about to pass the Big Daddy's, a voice in my head said, "Why not go in for a drink?" Which, for me, was extraordinary: never in my life had I gone to a bar for a solitary drink before. I ignored the thought and drove home.

On Tuesday night, the question came again: "Why not stop off for a drink?" And I asked myself if I was crazy to be having such a question-and-answer session in my own head.

On Wednesday night, the same question came a third time. (You know what it was.) And I gave up and submitted: I stopped and parked in front of the Big Daddy's, and went in.

Ruth was the bartender.

Astonishment on both sides - stories of personal events that separated her from Gainesville for a while, my efforts to find her. Bottom line: Ruth rejoined the cottage group, as if she had never been gone – and eventually became its leader.

But the question remains: what happened here? My personal analysis says that this was an advanced form of mental telepathy: subconscious on both our parts, operating at a distance. I knew I was looking for her, and she wanted to reintegrate with her old friends. Not enough to call me up, but subconsciously. So perhaps her spirit and my spirit linked up and decided they would do something about it. Or at least, so it seems to me.

BUILDING A MODEL

As I taught more classes, and as various unusual events (such as the above) happened, I was able to naturally build my own model as to how this could all work. I feel strongly that a basic model of how ESP works should have the following elements:

1. Be simple and understandable to most people. Explainable in 10-15 minutes, maximum.
2. Not cause any fear or inhibition. For example, the model shouldn't require we be super-human with exceptional genes.
3. Be a model that could be easily taught, could lower the barriers that prevent most people from disbelieving ESP events, and could lead to greater ESP participation.
4. ideally, one single model should be able to explain all ESP events. As a minimum, there shouldn't be different models for clairvoyance vs. telepathy; they should be related in some way.

The Silva Course did not teach a model of how this all worked. It simply provided tools that enabled us to succeed in a basic ESP experiment. The how's and why's were not addressed. But to some of us, the how's and why's are the most important parts of the equation – they might explain not just ESP, but the structure of our universe. (Not kidding here.) If we can be telepathic and clairvoyant, similar to radio and television, why can't we have precognition, too? And if we succeed in precognition, what does that tell us about time and the universe? Is everything and everybody going in a straight line from past, through present, and on to future? Or do all time dimensions co-exist, and we see time in our own way because of the limitations of our bodies or minds?

To me, those are the most interesting questions. In my Silva Course teaching days, I found that the unexpected event, such as finding Ruth, were the glimmers of the real power in ESP. There weren't a lot of stories, and I refused to seriously consider events that were confusing or ambiguous. I only paid attention when events happened that were clearly unusual, and which required explanations involving an ESP perspective.

There weren't a lot of events that fit these requirements. But they did happen, and I found that they happened more and more frequently as my Silva teaching continued. I wasn't practicing techniques daily or seeking out unusual events; I was simply teaching the course and leading my life. And, of course, I was open to allowing these events to happen – perhaps the most important requirement.

Apparently the constant immersion in the teaching and practice sessions made me more sensitive than I was prior. It wasn't an on / off switch; instead, it was like a sensitivity dial that set itself higher. It opened the possibility of new experiences.

THE MODEL THAT DEVELOPED FROM THESE EXPERIENCES

Each experience was a peek into ESP. Putting them together into a model might convey something to you, the reader; it did to me. This model resembles an early way of organizing computers in a network, used extensively in large corporations, called Distributed Data Processing. It involves the idea of "partitions".

Imagine that there is a large computer, for example one that runs retail grocery stores across the USA. Each store would use the same programs, but each store would have its own data. This data would be kept in a partition of its own, with links to the central partition that holds the company's programs:

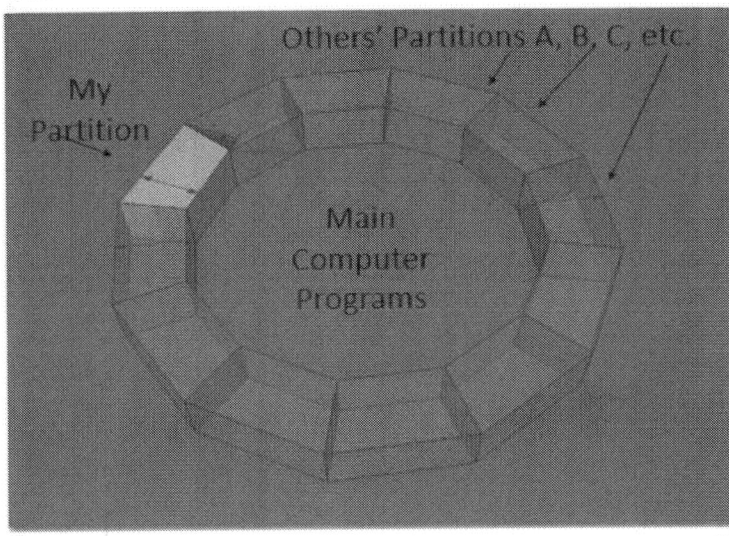

The key to this model is that all of the partitions and main program area are at a central location, the "mainframe". There are a number of local things that the store needs to do such as payroll, but there is a lot of work that requires more computing power. Such a case would be warehouse inventory replenishment (where I programmed), which applied various analytical models to predict the next week's consumer buying behavior. When a store is processing new orders, the mainframe's models are applied, the right model(s) selected, then new buy orders are issued for the next week's needs. These orders originate at the mainframe, go through communications lines, and emerge at the local computer where they are printed.

The point here is that our brain can be seen like that local computer, doing local programming tasks (e.g., keeping our heart beating and our lungs breathing). But when some serious "computing power" is needed, our brains communicate with a higher level of functioning.

Note that the higher functions of our minds – deep memory, creativity, telepathy clairvoyance and others – work in a similar way. They all involve:

1. Relaxing
2. Often casting our eyes upwards (such as when trying to remember something)
3. Imagining a visual image in our minds
4. And sometimes listening. (I had one of the most creative ideas of my career happen via a question that was asked in my mind, like a voice. The question led to a new software program approach that saved 3 years out of a budgeted 3.5 years for developing new software product.)

Normally, we go through our lives thinking in "our partition". We have private thoughts that drive our actions, our opinions and everything else about our lives. Yet once in a while, we "hear" something from another partition – maybe it's the thought that someone is going to telephone us (and they do five minutes later), maybe it's a cry for help from someone in trouble. It could be anything, but the key thing is it is not information from our own partition. This is very similar to a local computer going to the mainframe for a higher level of data or information processing.

There is one last feature of this model: each partition is complete and separate from the others, but sometimes there can be "leakage". Envision this like not having a ceiling in the partition, so we could hear a shout coming from another partition. That shout would have to be loud – "I'm drowning!!!" or "I'm trapped!!! Please help me!!!" – for us to hear it from someone else's partition.

Beyond the model, it is important to think about psychic functioning and its implications. ***If we ever, even once, hear information from another partition – that is, if we ever function telepathically – then it proves that it can be done. And once we know it can be done once, it can be done again.*** With practice, it may even become easier.

Living in the 21st century, it should be easier to believe in telepathy and clairvoyance since we grew up with radio and television. If engineers can make sounds and images travel through the air, why can't we do that through our "personal ether"?

And what is this personal ether? Perhaps it's our relationship with another person. A well-known fact: The closer the relationship between people, the easier it is for psychic events to happen between them.

As far as precognition goes, I don't have an easy explanation. The statement that "The partition holds all information – past, present and future" is not sufficient – it just begs the question. The same for telekinesis, moving objects by force of mind, which I have never experienced.

But telepathy and clairvoyance can be explained in this way. If we accept this explanation, it leads to a very serious question: Who wrote the rules, the program that allows this to happen? And that was the question that led me to believe in God's literal existence.

STORY: WHAT'S IN A NAME?

Many years ago, just after getting married, my wife and I were driving in Boston. It was a beautiful night, with a full moon and clear skies. We were all dressed up for a party, and she looked particularly beautiful. So beautiful that I said, "You look very beautiful tonight. You know, you don't look like an Irene – you look more like a Monique."

My wife gasped and seemed to turn pale, all of a sudden. She explained to me that, all during her childhood and adolescence, she imagined herself as a beautiful woman named Monique – and it was something she never told anyone. She was feeling quite beautiful that night, and it's possible that my mind picked up her internal association with the name Monique. As for me, that name had no particular meaning in my life.

What's particularly interesting is that this event happened fifteen years before I took the Silva Course.

WHAT DOES THIS ALL MEAN? WHAT LESSONS CAN WE LEARN?

The first possibility is that all this means nothing and that it's all self-deception. There are many people who still cling to this explanation. I don't believe that, and I do believe that such stories are not happening randomly without any cause or mechanism. I believe there is a communications channel between people, and even between people and animals. A case could even be made for communication with inanimate matter, as the following true story may suggest:

STORY: THE SWIMMING HOLE

After college, I returned to Boston, my home town. Soon after my return, I visited my brother and his family in Sudbury in the western suburbs. I drove a back route and drove past many, many cars parked in an unlikely place, with many teenagers going in the same direction in their bathing suits. So, feeling curious, I went the same way – and discovered a swimming hole that they all were using. It was in a beautiful place, surrounded by trees, and truly a special spot. I said to myself, "I'd like to buy that property and build a house here, someday."

Then I drove away. Unfortunately, I did not have the resources to buy that the land.

Six years later, I was in law school. Sitting in class one day, I thought of the swimming hole and how beautiful it had been. Sigh....

Then, the next day, the same thought came to me again. Another sigh....

And on the third day, a Friday, again the same thought of the swimming hole. "What's going on here?" I thought. By this time, I had taken and instructed the Silva course, and thought something psychic might be happening. So I hopped in my car after classes and drove out to Sudbury.

There was now a FOR SALE sign on the property where the swimming hole was located, and nailed on top of it was a very clean, fresh sign that said SOLD. It couldn't have been there a long time, and I guess I missed the opportunity to buy it very recently. Perhaps even during the past week when I had thoughts about the swimming hole.

What happened? Did the land call out to me, since I was the person with such a deep and close respect for it? Or did my mind just "tune in" to conversations between people about the property with the swimming hole? I'll never know. But the first option raises some interesting possibilities.

This could have been a telepathic or a clairvoyant experience (communicating with people vs with the land). It definitely was an unusual event. But note that it was my own, inner experience. I can never prove I had those thoughts, and this experience would be meaningless for a scientific observer. But it did happen, and it raises some interesting questions.

FOR THE SCIENTIFIC THINKERS:

For the scientific thinkers among us, this book may be disappointing. The Scientific Method, or the Aristotelian Method, requires that all experiments be externally observable and repeatable. Unfortunately, psychic events don't follow that rule.

Psychic functioning is an internal experience. Only you, the actor in the scene, know that you experienced what you described. Only you know if you are lying or not, or if there was a scam going on. For the scientist, that fails the test.

One famous scientist, Dr. J.B. Rhine of Duke University, approached the subject of ESP on a statistical basis: he had subjects guess what was on special "ESP cards" or "Zener cards" (also called "Rhine cards"). These cards had five designs on them, five of each for a pack of 25. The designs were:

Rhine's theory was that psychics ("recipients") would score statistically higher than the norm on guessing which card was being viewed in another location by the other participant (the "sender"). He reported success in his efforts, but his procedures were criticized by many scientists in later years. For more information, see Wikipedia's article on Extrasensory Perception. (https://en.wikipedia.org/wiki/Extrasensory_perception).

Thus, to date no one has been able to replicate or prove the existence (or non-existence) of extrasensory perception, ESP. Personally, I believe it exists but that it is episodic and not able to be performed on command. The Silva Course health cases are the best evidence I have been able to find. And my opinion is scientifically doubtful, since I was involved either as a participant or guide.

With ESP only you, the potential psychic, can know if you really saw what you reported. Scientific rules don't apply. Often, the demand for objectivity and non-involvement may prevent the experiment from being successful.

A POSSIBLE THEORY OF INTELLENCE

We are all taught that ideas are "in our head" – and by that, people literally mean within the physical space of our skulls. The ideas are contained inside our brains. On the other hand, most everyone accepts that there is a difference between the brain and the mind. To demonstrate: how much does a brain weigh? About 3 pounds. Now, how much does the mind weigh? Nearly everyone agrees that the mind does not have a weight. So what is it? And where does it exist? Is it merely a thought, like any other – or is the mind some special structure that exists beyond three dimensions?

And what about ideas: are all ideas formed inside the space within our skull? Are they kept there, like computer memory? What happens when we forget information – yet later on it reappears in our minds? Was it just lost inside our brains?

My personal belief, following the model I have described above, is that higher-level information – which includes ideas – come from our own "partition". This exists in another dimension, combined with mental processing that functions in that dimension. The role of our brain, beyond the "local functions" necessary for life, is to be a communicating device to access that data and those programs. It's a long-range transceiver (transmitter and receiver) crossing the dimensional divide. It functions automatically when we need it, and we don't have to understand how it works to make it work.

Let me suggest a "ladder of intelligence", going from what is familiar to what is not familiar:

1. Memory
2. Genius
3. Creativity
4. Telepathy
5. Clairvoyance
6. Precognition
7. Omniscience (for saints and gurus only)

There is, of course, intelligence that we use at the basic, physical level – the intelligence we need for everyday functioning. This would be similar to the local computer in the retail food store example – doing things that require no higher-level intelligence. The above list only shows levels of higher intelligence, beyond the physical.

In summary, this is the key concept of this model: our brain has two functions, just like the local computer in model described above:

a. Local functioning – supporting our physical needs, working with short-term memory requests. One local function might be playing baseball.
b. Communicating with our higher-level intelligence. Sometimes that information can be shared via telepathy, clairvoyance, etc.

This means that our brains incorporate a "multidimensional communicator" as part of their design. A device similar to radio or television that can go beyond the five senses of sight, hearing, taste, smell and feel. When we need to function in this way, our brains automatically make a request for this information. We don't know what it is, where it is, but it works when we need it. To access the information, we have to make the request in the right way.

What is the right way? A lot of ESP research says that the following are required:

1. Relaxation, including slow breathing and heart rate. This leads to a slowing of our brain waves, ideally to the 14 cycles per second range, known as Alpha waves. Apparently, this frequency is more efficient for ESP function.
2. Focusing our thoughts on what we need, preferably in an image. (Advanced users can also make requests conceptually, after a lot of practice with image-based functioning.)
3. Focusing our will strongly on the request made – asking for it, wanting it, needing it, demanding it even. That force of will makes our request more like a shout in the "personal ether".
4. Keeping our minds focused and listening or viewing our inner senses to receive a response.
5. Not thinking about how this request can be achieved, only on the end-goal we seek. If we focus on the how, we get stuck in things that we believe are possible and impossible, which then blocks our strength of will. Just let it happen.

Sounds a lot like prayer, you say? Well, it is prayer – among other things. The only difference is that we do not have to ask it from God, unless we choose to. Our multi-channel / multi-dimensional communicator sends the request out in ways we don't understand or know, and sometimes we get a response.

> Think about the story "Where's Ruth?", above. Every effort I made to find her sent out such a request. My answer came in the form of a question in my mind: "Why don't you go in for a drink?" and when I did, Ruth was the bartender – almost seeming to wait for me.

Now we can look at the higher levels of intelligence from this perspective:

MEMORY: We are making a simple request to access facts that we have personally experienced and which are already stored in our partition (short-term memory). When asked a question needing a deeper memory request, we often raise our eyes above the horizon. This triggers Alpha brainwave activity, which is the "communications frequency" – it allows us to receive information from our partition.

GENIUS: When a moment of genius comes, it can be of two forms:

1. Genius based on information already in our experience. Here, we take the facts already in our partition and apply advanced analysis to it, at a subconscious level. We can get new solutions this way – sometimes, perhaps occasionally or even frequently depending on our level of skill.
2. Genius based on a mixture of information we know and don't know. This is the next step, where we combine information known to us locally or in our partition, with information we "imagine" – information from other partitions, or perhaps information that simply exists elsewhere. There's no proof for this theorem, but my belief is that this is another level of request, originating from our own knowledge partition, and asking for help from other partitions of information. And sometimes it comes through. Thomas Edison's dreams (you can Google the phrase) is an example of this type of functioning.

CREATIVITY: This is a more free-form version of genius, where we seek new ideas without necessarily rooting them in information we have experienced. Here is where the requests become are more conceptual and not rooted in our own experience. Salvador Dali's surrealistic art could serve as an example of this, but millions of other examples are all around us. If you think back to the best idea of your life, ask yourself how it came to you. Often, it just "appeared". My proposition is that it was being worked on at a subconscious level (facts known to you + facts coming through this communications channel). All that is needed is an idea request broadcast on your channel for an idea on a specific subject.

TELEPATHY: Here we go to our partition and try to communicate with another partition – either facts in that partition (a health case in the Silva Course) or the person connected to that partition (knowing when a friend will telephone you). It's like being in a closed room, but hearing voices from others in their own rooms nearby.

CLAIRVOYANCE: Seeing a complete situation as if in a picture. The situation could be anything, anywhere, anytime. The hard problem is finding a situation that can be verified as accurate. This occasionally happens, as with a Silva health case which is designed to have feedback available from someone in your class. Or you might dream of a number which turns out to be a lottery (almost) winner. It could be past or present, or perhaps even future – it is impossible to know while seeing that image exactly when it is. (When the card's writer, a relative of the health subject, asked me to go back and view the calendar on the wall, it was a brilliant solution to this problem.)

PRECOGNITION: Seeing something before it happens? How can that be? I don't know how it happens, but it does sometimes happen. It suggests that the data in our partition is data from all of Time, not just what we have experienced in the past. This is a very advanced topic, and it may be decades before there is serious research on this subject. Some folks are thinking about it today, however, such as Adam Frank:

> In relativity theory the past, present and future *already* exist in the four-dimensional continuum of space-time. You *think* next Tuesday hasn't occurred yet. But in relativity, every event in your life defines a single 4-D object called your world-line and it's all there already.

Physicists, however, are sure this "block universe" of relativity is not the whole story.

Space-time must, at the smallest scales, become *quantized,* like sand on the beach. Hunting for quantum versions of space-time, scientists are now in remarkable territory. It's a place where time as a fundamental actor in physics may fade away. Time might be *emergent* — a derived aspect of a more fundamental and timeless reality.

More radical ideas reject the notion of time altogether, taking each moment as separate and eternal.

Perhaps the *now* is all that exists, the past and future merely illusions. Or, perhaps, it is the *now* that's an illusion and below the appearance of change is a timeless substrate that is perfect in its eternal repose.

One thing is, however, certain. Looking across the broad field of human endeavor — science, art and religion — time and the question of its illusion remains essential, and essentially unresolved.

Our days certainly *seem* numbered. We long to know if this countdown to darkness is real, or simply the trick of a more limited perspective.

You can keep up with more of what Adam Frank is thinking on Facebook and Twitter. His new book is About Time: Cosmology and Culture at the Twilight of the Big Bang.

> *Source:* http://www.npr.org/sections/13.7/2011/11/08/142118441/is-time-an-illusion-from-the-buddha-to-brian-greene (emphasis supplied)

Whoever you are, I can guarantee that thinking about Time will be confusing. Here's my simple take on the subject: Whatever Time is, it's probably beyond any simple description you can read here. Our inability to see the higher aspects of Time comes from our souls' existence in a three-dimensional, physical body that lives in a past-present-future timeline. That is, our ability to see beyond the three dimensions (or four, if you see past-present-future as a dimension) is limited by the mental constructs we have built to live in this 3-D world. Time in its totality is far beyond that, but we are unable to see it, except for a few of us (who are generally physicists and mathematicians) in limited ways.

> For a video description of these theories by, you might view The Illusion of Time, from the Fabric of the Cosmos series on NOVA (2011). This can be seen on YouTube at https://www.youtube.com/watch?v=9Qu9XaF2K10. It's hosted by Brian Greene, a physics professor at Columbia University. Time concepts are well explained with a lot of video support.

I can't promise that this theory of ESP is true. But I do believe that our physicality limits our perceptions. That is why we mentally "go to our level" to escape the physical world around us. We go to a mental, conceptual world where more possibilities exist. And there we make our multi-dimensional requests, if we have the presence of mind to do so. Sometimes we simply fall asleep in the middle of the meditation, and lose the opportunity.

OMNISCIENCE: This, of course, is the ultimate level, reserved to the Gods. This involves knowing one's own partition, having access to everyone else's and to the main computer programs in the mainframe –

and even access to whoever wrote the rules, in the first place. This is special beyond concept, and please give me a call if you get there. I want to join you.

SUMMARY OF ESP, THE PROPOSED MODEL AND HUMAN CAPABILITIES:

If you have had episodes of ESP, some of what I've written hopefully made sense to you. And if you have wondered about how it all fits together, hopefully again some of these writings make sense to you.

The conclusions I have made from building this model are the following:

- The mind has multi-dimensional communications capability. That part of the model is, for me at least, proven and accepted.
- Anyone can train capabilities to advance further along the higher-intelligence ladder. It's a basic human skill and capability. The only thing that will hold you back is if you don't believe it will work, and therefore it's not worth trying. The harder you try, the stronger your will to communicate, the better the success will be.
- The different elements of higher intelligence are simply steps along a path, skills that can be improved. If you have a good memory, you can probably expand that to genius-level thinking if you haven't already. Give it a chance and ask yourself challenging questions. Practice, practice, practice. No one else needs to know what you're trying to develop in your mind.
- Telepathy and clairvoyance are quite similar. Telepathy is just the stepping-off point, where we have limited ourselves to direct person-to-person communication. The next step, clairvoyance, advances your skillset and enlarges your ideas quite a bit.

- Don't worry about precognition – it will happen or not. I have no way to suggest training for it. Even so, not many people will believe you. (How did you react to my lottery story?)
- Omniscience? Forget about it.

I hope you have enjoyed these pages. I stand by everything I wrote. What I said I experienced, I did experience. The stories are all true and not exaggerated.

The question isn't whether you believe it all. The question is what you would do if it were all true. What would ***you*** do? Specifically? Why not go ahead and try it anyhow? Don't even bother with the belief question – just try it out. If you have success, belief will follow.

I can guarantee that if you have unusual experiences like the ones described, you definitely will open your mind to new ideas.

Isn't that what Life's all about?

Richard Tamir, September 2017

APPENDIX A: DESCRIPTION OF THE SILVA COURSE CURRICULUM

SOURCE: http://www.mindtosucceed.com/silva-method.html

SILVA LIFE SYSTEMS (SLS) CURRICULUM

PART 1 - HEALTH MANAGEMENT & STRESS CONTROL

- Train your mind to access the Alpha level easily. By the end of the Silva Method program you will be able to access very deep levels of mind in seconds.

- Insomnia remedy: How to use your mind to get you to drift off to sleep.

- How to program your brain to wake up without an alarm clock at whatever time you desire. This is a healthier alternative to a loud, heart-stopping alarm clock.

- How to erase a headache in seconds and a migraine in minutes.
- How to accelerate healing and control pain.
- How to re-energize and rejuvenate yourself in 60 seconds or less
-

PART 2 - MIND TRAINING

- A little trick to free yourself from negative thoughts and feelings.
- A simple method to measurably increase your focus and concentration.
- Gain self awareness by remembering dreams and using them for problem solving.
- How to run your brain's memory system so that you will never have to write a grocery list (or any other reminder list) ever again.
- Learn ANYTHING faster: how to reduce your study time by improving retention and recall of anything you read or hear.
- Erase test-taking anxiety with a simple process that makes recall during exams easier.

PART 3 - SUCCESS CONDITIONING

- Secrets of Powerful language: What to say, and what you must NEVER say, so that your brain AUTOMATICALLY solves problems and generates creative ideas.

- Improve communication and performance skills through mental conditioning.
- Discover the ultimate secret to "creative visualization." Mind Visualization is a VERY powerful tool, but most people leave out this one crucial step to making it work.
- Free yourself of unwanted habits. (Think you've got a tough habit, like overeating or smoking? This process has been proven effective for heroin addiction!)
- Deepen the connection and pleasure of ALL your relationships. Build better rapport with others and tap into their unspoken concerns.
- Program your subconscious mind for success.
- An easy formula for staying focused, positive and motivated.

PART 4 - PROBLEM SOLVING

- How to access your intuition in a moment to help you make the best decision.
- How to program your brain to find a workable solution to any problem using an ordinary glass of water.

MIND POWER TECHNIQUES TAUGHT OFFERED IN THE SILVA LIFE SYSTEMS ON DEMAND WEB COURSE:

- Sleep Control. A technique to fall and stay asleep throughout the night (without the use of drugs)

- Clock Technique, a mind power technique to master your use of time; wake up without an alarm and/or prevent jag lag
- To Awake Control - to energize yourself and/or stay awake longer without drowsiness
- Dream Control, subconscious mind power technique for problem solving
- Headache Control to stop headaches and stress related discomfort
- Mental Screen to improve visualization, creativity and problem solving
- Memory Pegs for improving memory, mind visualization and developing creativity
- Three Fingers Technique, a trigger or anchor that you can use with eyes open to access memory and resourceful states any time, anywhere
- Mirror of the Mind for focusing and manifesting goals. You can use this technique for reprogramming the subconscious mind to change limiting beliefs.
- Weight and Habit Control
- Hand Levitation for accessing deeper levels of mind. Used for mind body healing and reprogramming subconscious
- Glove Anesthesia for pain management
- Glass of Water problem solving technique
- Sensory projection through multidimensional "travel"
- Mental Laboratory and "counselors" for advanced problem solving

- Accessing higher levels of intelligence

Printed in Great Britain
by Amazon

34959246R00034